Implications for Hybrid Teleworking-Programs for Regeneration and Sustainable Development

A Booklet By:
Tanisha Beecher-Bell
Master of Adult & Community
Leadership Education

Implications for Hybrid Teleworking Programs for Regeneration and Sustainable Development

RSVIP Services, LLC

Copyright © 2020 by Tanisha Beecher Bell

https://www.rsvipllc.com/book-store
https://www.facebook.com/TanishaBeecherBell/
https://twitter.com/Author_Bell
https://www.instagram.com/author_beecherbell/
https://www.linkedin.com/company/rsvipbookstore/
https://www.youtube.com/channel/UCxVO5lYxb8-Kq1Jdwg97dBA
https://www.facebook.com/Tanisha.Beecher/

Implications for Hybrid Teleworking Programs for Regeneration and Sustainable Development

Table of Contents

Acknowledgement.........................Page 7
Introduction................................Page 9
Needs Assessment................................Page 15
Project Description
Action Plan:
    Project Purpose.................Page 25
    Project Vision....................Page 26
    Project Mission..................Page 26
Major Goal, Objectives and Measures...................................Page 27
The Hybrid Teleworking Educational Program Development.............................Page 34
Final Reflections..........................Page 41
Description of Project Design......................................Page 44
Collective Behaviors to Ensure Program Success...................................Page 48
Persons who are Most Likely to Work from Home................................Page 48
Social Implications for Hybrid Teleworking......................Page 54
Economic Implications for Hybrid

Implications for Hybrid Teleworking Programs for Regeneration and Sustainable Development

Teleworking Programs..................Page 59
Environmental Implications
for Hybrid
Teleworking Programs..................Page 62
References................................Page 64

Implications for Hybrid Teleworking Programs for Regeneration and Sustainable Development

Acknowledgement

I would like to extend my sincerest gratitude to my Sustainability Leadership Professor, Dr. John Hardman. You have taught us processes for going beyond conventional ways of thinking and acting, in efforts of adopting a deeper and more conscious approach within and outside of our organizations, to achieve real sustainable change. Thank you, Dr. Hardman, for your exceptional guidance and encouragement with this project.

Dr. Susan Dennett, thank you so much for being a truly inspiring leader and professor. You have made the Adult and Community Leadership Education Masters Program a most intellectually stimulating experience. The program has been pivotal for me, and I have found it to be most relevant to my life.

Thanks to you, readers, for allowing me to inspire you, through this book. I wish you all the best in your sustainable development journey. Please know that we are making this journey together.

Cheers to regeneration and sustainable development!

Tanisha Beecher Bell

Implications for Hybrid Teleworking Programs for Regeneration and Sustainable Development

Introduction

According to the Brundtland Report (1987), as cited by Hardman (2011), "sustainable development is deve-lopment that meets the needs of the present without compromising the ability of future generations to meet their own needs" (pg. 65).

The Regenerative Leadership Frame-work is a concept that shifts focus away from the consequences of our actions regarding sustainability, to the deve-lopment of higher levels of awareness resulting in behavioral change in favor of our natural and social environment. I'm reminded of my religion, in which, for some denominations, 'hell' is often conveyed as the consequence for not sharing the beliefs of those particular denominations, even though we serve the same God. This approach inadvertently frightens persons into converting. I personally believe that many efforts in life are more 'sustainable'

Implications for Hybrid Teleworking Programs for Regeneration and Sustainable Development

when they appeal to our personal sense of purpose, rather than something we fear or feel obligated to do.

A regenerative tool that I have found most powerful is the ability to sense the core values of the persons I'm engaging, so that I may successfully appeal to them. This is the most effective way to build a network and engage multiple stakeholders. "To embed sustainability in every human action as a natural rather than an artificial behavior, we must develop a more complete or integral vision of reality as it is, not as we think it is or are conditioned to see it," (Hardman, 2011, p.33).

The strategy for informally engaging multiple stakeholders on the subject of sustainability is becoming increasingly popular throughout the corporate world. Commitment to multiple stakeholder engagement can help us achieve the triple top line on a global scale. The triple top line:

Implications for Hybrid Teleworking Programs for Regeneration and Sustainable Development

"How to grow prosperity, celebrate community and enhance the health of all species for all time" (Cuginotti, Miller, & van der Pluijm, 2008, as cited by Hardman, 2011, p. 10).

More countries will be able to appreciate and experience peace of mind, a healthier environment, as well as prosperity. For instance, an international regeneration group, the Savory Institute, which was established in 2009, engages leaders and entrepreneurs internationally, to promote regeneration in agriculture such as agro-ecology and cover cropping. Such alliances are great examples of how many leaders are attempting to balance their personal needs with the greater common good.

Based on my observation, experience, and research, the COVID-19 pandemic has significantly changed the way we live, particularly the way we do business. The recent lockdowns resulted in either

Implications for Hybrid Teleworking Programs for Regeneration and Sustainable Development

employees losing their jobs, or being offered the opportunity to temporarily work from home. Nevertheless, these options have caused positive changes for the environment, but we have also witnessed the negative economic impacts. As we go forward as a community, we must ask ourselves: Would it be feasible and beneficial to permanently implement teleworking as a viable means of achieving regeneration and sustainable development? This education program will cover the economic, environmental and social implications for teleworking.

The recent COVID-19 pandemic has contributed to global financial crisis, and has definitely quickened the momentum of a shift towards working from home. This education program may serve as a crucial one-stop starting point for businesses and citizens who are considering their options for teleworking. "Given the important connection between our working lives and our economic lives, we must try to understand the workforce of the future," (Donovan, 2016).

The notion of teleworking is not new, however, implementing a better and more thoroughly researched approach will be much appreciated in the near future. There are jobs that do not need people to be in a physical office with others, and the reduction in time on the road could lead to significant increases in productivity, as well as reduction in emissions from vehicles. Teleworking has the added benefit of reduced consumption and waste of many office supplies such as paper. There is also the significant savings in reduced office space, facilities maintenance and waste management.

The concept of regenerative leadership "is applied by formal and informal leaders at all levels of organizations who engage groups of people in the development of higher

Implications for Hybrid Teleworking Programs for Regeneration and Sustainable Development

levels of awareness that translate into behaviors that seek not merely to preserve existing natural and social resources while ensuring a healthy bottom line, but to restore and create new resources that have become depleted through overuse or misuse" (Hardman, 2011). This education plan is relevant and will deepen our understanding of regeneration and sustainable development. It will also increase our awareness of our interconnectedness to the world around us. Together we can work towards developing habits of continuously balancing the benefits of actions between personal interest and the greater common good.

Implications for Hybrid Teleworking Programs for Regeneration and Sustainable Development

Needs Assessment that Led to the Reason for the Education Plan

The assessment targeted 25 adults including male and female. However, only 17 of 25 willingly participated. At times, persons were either very cautious about their responses, or very defensive. A questionnaire was administered in person and/or over the phone to 17 participants including local business and citizens during the COVID-19 crisis. The questionnaire targeted the likelihood that participants would adapt to the idea of hybrid teleworking programs and the factors that influence the decision to do so. The questions are as follows:

1. What does sustainability mean to you?
2. Do you have concerns about remaining operable during times of crisis?
3. Does your firm support efforts of minimizing commute, such as car pooling and working from home?

Implications for Hybrid Teleworking Programs for Regeneration and Sustainable Development

4. Do you feel that hybrid teleworking programs could help the environment, and why?
5. Do you feel that implementation of a hybrid teleworking program is feasible for your business/organization, and why?
6. What would you consider to be the benefits of working from home?
7. What would you consider to be the downside to working from home?
8. On a scale of 1 - 5 with 1 being highly un-necessary and 5 being highly necessary, please rate your perception of the necessity for hybrid teleworking programs.
9. On a scale of 1 – 5 with 1 being the lowest and 5 being the highest, please rate your perception of whether working from home gives a sense of greater independence.
10. On a scale of 1 – 5 with 1 being the lowest and 5 being the highest, please rate your perception of

whether working from home reduces overall stress levels.

For this mixed methods research, interviews were conducted with local citizens and businesses, as a means of engaging the community and creating a network for promoting the educational program. Based on the results from the needs assessment, the researcher found that majority of civilians perceive that teleworking programs could help the environment; improve work-life balance; reduce overall stress levels; improve job security. Teleworking programs are perceived as being necessary. The community is therefore opened to the Hybrid Teleworking for Regeneration and Sustainable Development Education Program.

Further research was carried out through examination of existing literature to explore the social, environmental and economical implications for hybrid teleworking.

Findings:

Question #1:
What does sustainability mean to you?
Common recurring themes include:
- Relates to climate change
- Recycling
- Saving the planet
- Reducing pollution
- Planting trees
- Driving electric vehicles
- Reducing waste

Question#2:
Do you have concerns about remaining operable during times of crisis?

Of the 17 participants, 12 indicated concerns about remaining operable. The majority was concerned about remaining profitable, retaining their employees and keeping them paid.

Five participants either indicated that they were more frustrated than concerned, or had no comments at the moment.

Question #3:
Does your firm support efforts of minimizing commute, such as car pooling and working from home?

4 out 17 participants reported involvement in some efforts to minimize commute. One of the 4 indicated more than 80 percent switch to a flexible workplace program. Two retail store managers shared that they had already switched to a virtual platform so that cashiers and other workers could provide customer service through online chat, and telephone. One participant stated that prior to COVID-19, she carpooled with colleagues, as well as utilized public transportation but no longer did so

in adherence to social distancing guidelines.

The remaining participants either indicated that their employer did not support efforts of minimizing commute, or saw no environmental benefits in doing so.

Question #4:
Do you feel that hybrid teleworking programs could help the envi-ronment, and why?

Of the 17 participants, 12 of them indicated yes. Common recurring themes as to why are:
- Personalized schedule
- Less traffic
- Less congestion
- Less emissions from non-hybrid and non electric-vehicles
- Reduced carbon foot-print

- Opportunity to wear robe & house-slippers all day

The remaining 5 participants either did not think that teleworking would have a significant enough effect, if any at all, on the environment, but would help economically during times of crisis.

Question #5:
Do you feel that implementation of a hybrid teleworking program is feasible for your business/organization, and why?

Of 17 participants, 9 were confident that some form of flexibility would be feasible within their workplace. Common recurring themes as to why:

- Already involved in some form of telework
- Some employees were not always physically

> needed at the office and could work from home.
> - Already seeking strategies for remaining operable and gaining competitive advantage during a crisis.

Three participants were unsure; one participant felt that with a little push management could find a way, three participants did not wish to comment now.

Question #6:
What would you consider to be the benefits of working from home?

Recurring themes include:
- Savings on gas purchase
- Reduced road rage
- Reduced stress
- Reduced disruptions from work colleagues
- Improved work-life balance

Question #7: What would you consider to be the downside of working from home?

Recurring themes include:
- Reduced mental stimulation
- Lack of being seen
- Lack of new knowledge
- Feeling cut off from the world
- Boredom from lack of co-worker engagement
- Absence of separation between home and work life
- Sense of reduced job security

Question #8:
On a scale of 1 - 5 with 1 being highly unnecessary and 5 being highly necessary, please rate your perception of the necessity for hybrid teleworking programs.

Of the 17 participants, 12 gave a rating of 3 or higher, indicating they perceive that there is a necessity for hybrid teleworking programs.

Question #9:

On a scale of 1 – 5 with 1 being the lowest and 5 being the highest, please rate your perception of whether working from home gives a sense of greater independence.

Of the 17 participants, 13 (76%) gave a rating of 3 or higher, indicating that they perceive that working from home may give a sense of greater independence.

Question #10:

On a scale of 1 – 5 with 1 being the lowest and 5 being the highest, please rate your perception of whether working from home reduces overall stress levels.

Of the 17 participants, 14 (82%) of them gave a rating of 3 or higher, indicating that they perceive that working from home reduces overall stress levels.

Implications for Hybrid Teleworking Programs for Regeneration and Sustainable Development

Project Description and Action Plan

Purpose: Hardman (2011) has determined that the Regenerative Leadership Framework is "applied by formal and informal leaders at all levels of organizations who engage groups of people in the development of higher levels of awareness that translate into behaviors that seek not merely to preserve existing natural and social resources while ensuring a healthy bottom line, but to restore and create new resources that have become depleted through overuse or misuse."

The purpose of this initiative is to provide local businesses and citizens of Broward County, with the opportunity to learn about the implications for implementing hybrid teleworking (working from home) programs as a viable strategy for achieving regeneration and sustainable development.

Implications for Hybrid Teleworking Programs for Regeneration and Sustainable Development

Program Vision: To foster purpose-driven transformational leadership by engaging leaders and the community to utilize hybrid teleworking programs as a strategy for pollution prevention and social wellbeing.

Program Mission: To utilize the Regenerative Leadership Framework to achieve the triple top line by gradually securing the buy-in of organizations, County leaders, and fellow citizens, in support and implementation of hybrid teleworking programs.

Implications for Hybrid Teleworking Programs for Regeneration and Sustainable Development

Major Goal & Objectives: This educational program provides a means through which persons can shift the focus away from the consequences of their actions regarding sustainability, to the development of higher levels of awareness resulting in behavioral change in favor of our natural and social environment.

The overarching goal is to provide an opportunity for local businesses and citizens of Broward County to enhance their core knowledge of regenerative sustainability through this Regenerative Sustainability Educational Program. Scharmer (2007), as cited by Hardman (2011), states that presencing, "the ability to sense and bring into the present one's highest potential- as an individual and as a group, is an approach that brings leaders together to limit the possible negative outcomes of long-term forecasting." This educational program will utilize presencing to engage multiple stakeholders in achieving mutual exploration and engagement.

Table 1: Program Objectives and PIs

Program Objectives	Performance Indicators
Establish a Regenerative Sustainability platform through which multiple stakeholders will be engaged.	Regenerative Sustainability education program published by December 01, 2021.
Engage, recruit and train program volunteers.	Minimum of three program volunteers recruited by December 31, 2022.
Achieve 75% increased awareness on regenerative sustainability.	75% of the people engaged report increased awareness on regenerative sustainability as of

Implications for Hybrid Teleworking Programs for Regeneration and Sustainable Development

	December 31, 2023.
Achieve 75% increased knowledge on the implications for hybrid teleworking programs.	75% of total engaged persons report increased knowledge on the implications for hybrid teleworking programs as of January 30, 2024.
Engage/introduce program to two key representatives of Broward County Go Green Team.	Two key representatives of the Broward County Go Green Team engaged by January 30, 2023.
Engage/introduce program to two key representatives from Broward County's Pollution Prevention Division.	Two key representatives from Broward County's Pollution Prevention Division engaged by February 28, 2023.

Implications for Hybrid Teleworking Programs for Regeneration and Sustainable Development

Engage/introduce program to a representative of the Office of Economic and Small Business Development of Broward County.	One representative of the Office of Economic and Small Business Development of Broward County engaged by February 28, 2023.
Participate in a minimum of two sustainable outreach events each month.	Sustainability events attended at least twice per month as of March 1, 2023.
Obtain program approval and adoption by Broward County Board of County Commissioners.	Program approved and adopted by Broward County Government by June 30, 2024.
Achieve 10% increase in the number of good days per month	Achieved 10% increase in the number of good

reflected on the Broward County Air Quality Index Report, beginning September 30, 2022.	days per month reflected on Broward County Air Quality Index Report, beginning September 30, 2025.
Achieve 10% increase in the number of teleworkers who report greater satisfaction with their work commutes.	Achieved 10% increase in the number of teleworkers who report greater satisfaction with their work commutes as of October 1, 2025.
Engage in continuous marketing activities to gain raise awareness and gain supporters/followers.	❖ Created a minimum of three social marketing platforms, as of April 1, 2022 to be

	utilized for marketing and outreach. ❖ Gained a minimum of 5 new followers each month beginning May 1, 2022. ❖ Gained a minimum of 20% increased web traffic on a quarterly basis as of July 1, 2025.
Acquire a minimum of 5 local business	A minimum of 5 local businesses

Implications for Hybrid Teleworking Programs for Regeneration and Sustainable Development

participants per month.	successfully registered for the program each month, as of December, 2025
Achieve 10% increase in the number of leaders reporting improved leadership style.	A minimum of 5 local businesses successfully registered for the program each month, as of December 2025.

Implications for Hybrid Teleworking Programs for Regeneration and Sustainable Development

The Hybrid Teleworking Educational Program Development

The Hybrid Teleworking Educational Program for Regeneration and Sustainable Development will be officially published by RSVIP Services, LLC, and made available for purchase through a number of online platforms.

Once three volunteers have been hired, professional influence will be utilized to secure virtual and or in-person meetings with the Office of Economic and Small Business Development, Broward County Go Green Section, and Broward County Environmental Engineering Permitting Division, on behalf of Fresh Air, Inc. The purpose of the meetings is to introduce and present this educational program.

Buy-in from either or all of the key members identified could mean possible adoption of the program by County

Implications for Hybrid Teleworking Programs for Regeneration and Sustainable Development

Commissioners and small businesses within Broward County.

In addition, pertinent information regarding sustainability events and programs within Broward will be gathered for the purpose of continuous multiple stakeholder engagement.

The concept of regenerative sustainability "is applied by formal and informal leaders at all levels of organizations who engage groups of people in the development of higher levels of awareness that translate into behaviors that seek not merely to preserve existing natural and social resources while ensuring a healthy bottom line, but to restore and create new resources that have become depleted through overuse or misuse" (Hardman, 2011).

The Researcher's role in this program is to facilitate implementation and help bring awareness to both the program and the concept of regeneration and sustainable development.

Seeking buy-in from key stakeholders so that objectives can be achieved, and expected outcomes realized by of December 31, 2025. At this time a summative evaluation will be conducted by examining performance measures to determine achievement of program objectives. The results will be posted on the website as well as social media.

During in-person presentations the observation method will be used to help gain a sense of how to successfully connect with leaders and participants emotionally and financially, in an effort to attain mutual exploration and engagement during the presentations. This style of engagement is referred to as presencing, a blending of 'presence' and 'sensing', which is the ability to sense and bring into the present one's highest future potential—as an individual and as a group" (Hardman, 2011).

The program will implore leaders and participants to apply the following steps from the Sustainability Pyramid:
  i. Share information about the challenges they have identified with employing the program.
  ii. Explore the causes for these challenges.
  iii. Brainstorm ideas for improvement of the challenges.
  iv. Plan on implementing the improvement.
  v. Commit to the improvement; thus committing to implementing the program where applicable.

Training pre-test
  i. Do you have knowledge about regenerative sustainability?
  ii. Do you feel that carbon emissions cause of air pollution?

Implications for Hybrid Teleworking Programs for Regeneration and Sustainable Development

Training post-test

i. On a scale of 1-5, with 1 being strongly disagree and 5 being strongly agree, please rate your level of agreement with the statement: "I have gained greater knowledge about regenerative sustainability."

ii. On a scale of 1-5, with 1 being strongly disagree and 5 being strongly agree, please rate your level of agreement with the statement: "I have gained greater knowledge about the implications for teleworking as strategy for regenerative sustainability."

iii. On a scale of 1-5, with 1 being strongly disagree and 5 being strongly agree, please rate your level of agreement with the statement: "I have the capacity to support the project by setting aside my personal agenda."

iv. Do you intend to change your behavior in the future by applying

> the regenerative concepts outlined in the training?

Transfer of Learning

A Teleworking Dashboard will be available for public tracking of local businesses and organizations' parti-cipation in the teleworking movement.

Follow-up emails will be sent intermittently to participants inquiring as to whether they have explored the idea of teleworking by applying the steps from the Pyramid Lite. A post-course questionnaire will be provided to training session participants one month after the presentation, to help determine if the training was relevant and if transfer of learning occurred. A satisfactory survey will also be provided to gain a sense of employees' level of satisfaction with applicable teleworking programs.

Employee Satisfaction Survey

　　i.　Do you currently engage in teleworking?

　　ii.　On a scale of 1-5 with one being strongly dissatisfied and 5 being strongly satisfied, please rate your level of satisfaction with the teleworking program.

　　iii.　What do you like the least about teleworking?

　　iv.　What do you like the most about teleworking?

Implications for Hybrid Teleworking Programs for Regeneration and Sustainable Development

Final Reflections

Personal: The project design will help boost my knowledge of core sustainability concepts, and awareness of relevant current issues and trends. It involves engagement of multiple stakeholders and deep listening, which will improve my ability to interact more competently with professionals and experts.

As a result of this program participants will achieve:

1. Greater understanding of the Regenerative Leadership Framework
2. Increased core knowledge of regeneration and sustainable development
3. Greater understanding of the implications for implementing a hybrid teleworking program.
4. Increased motivation to engage like-minded leaders on the topic

of regeneration sustainable development.
5. Increased motivation to introduce or raise the topic of regeneration in meetings and conversations.
6. Increased number of employees who work from home as a result of the implementation of permanent hybrid teleworking programs.
7. Increased numbers of employees who are more satisfied with their work commute as a result of hybrid teleworking.

The program has the potential of being utilized and further developed by business and government organizations on a national scale. The marketing strategy as well as multiple stakeholder engagement could result in adoption and further development by businesses and government organizations on a global scale. Leaders are

Implications for Hybrid Teleworking Programs for Regeneration and Sustainable Development

now finding ways to engage multiple stakeholders and inspiring others to believe that there is power in the choices that we make in our individual lives on a daily basis. "Just one action by you, multiplied by millions, is a shift," (Kyte, as cited by Hyon, 2019).

Description of the Project Design

The Integrated Design Process will be utilized to engage and collaborate with key stakeholders, such as local entrepreneurs, community groups and governmental agencies such as the Pollution Prevention Division. Regenerative conversations will be held regarding development of the most efficient and effective means for rolling out respective teleworking programs, and empowering other communities and businesses to develop sustainable solutions. This can be achieved through the following, which was developed from aspects of the Sustainable Value Framework identified by Senge et al (2008), as cited by Hardman (2011, p. 207):

- ❖ External Strategy Today:
    - ○ Collaborate with stakeholders to achieve the most effective and efficient implementation process. The

payoff for this would include legitimacy.
- ❖ Internal Strategy Today:
  - ○ Collaborate with stakeholders on Pollution prevention through reduction in emissions. The payoff would be cost reduction and increased job security.

- ❖ External Strategy Tomorrow:
  - ○ Collaborate with stakeholders to create a shared roadmap to meet unmet needs. Payoff would be increased awareness and growth in regeneration and sustainable development.
- ❖ Internal Strategy of Tomorrow:
  Development of sustainable competencies of future payoff would include

increased employee loyalty and increased profitability.

Roles and Positions

- ❖ Tanisha Beecher-Bell, (the researcher), will serve as a Part-time Program Director, in charge of facilitating implementation and helping bring awareness to both the program and the concept of regeneration and sustainable development.
- ❖ Volunteers:
    - One part-time Administrative Assistant: Provides clerical and administrative assistance to the rest of the team.
    - One part-time Marketing Coordinator: In charge of overseeing all marketing related activities.
    - One Part-time Outreach Coordinator: In charge of organizing and overseeing

outreach and fund-raising activities.

Stakeholders

- ❖ Program Director and volunteers will work together to acquire buy-in from the following prospective stakeholders:
    - ○ Community groups
    - ○ Small business owners
    - ○ Broward County Go Green Team
    - ○ Broward County Pollution Prevention Division
    - ○ Office of Economic and Small Business Development of Broward County
    - ○ Broward County Board of County Commissioners

Implications for Hybrid Teleworking Programs for Regeneration and Sustainable Development

Collective Systems and Behaviors to Ensure Program Success

The behaviors necessary to ensure the program's success include:

- ❖ Willingness to engage in deep listening in an effort to be more opened to change and new processes.
- ❖ Willingness to engage with other organizations and community groups.
- ❖ The practice of inclusivity in the decision-making process.
- ❖ Awareness of the interconnectedness of society, the economy and wellbeing.

Persons who are Most Likely to Work from Home

The U.S. Department of Labor defines teleworking, which includes telecommuting, as working from home or an approved remote site, outside of an employer's place of business. Teleworking includes the use of telephones, computer software, and the Internet. Teleworkers are employees who work from home or an approved remote site, full-time or part-time. Teleworking can potentially be identified with the triple-top line, a regenerative concept, which, according to Hardman (2011), poses the question: "How can I grow prosperity, celebrate my community, and enhance the health of all species?" Although the concept of teleworking is not new, it has not been very popular among organizations.

According to the 2019 National Compensation Survey from the Bureau of Labor and Statistics, only a fraction of our nation's approximated 140 million workers currently have access to telework. According to the Time Use Survey from the U.S. Bureau of Labor Statistics (2020), "24 percent of employed persons in 2019 did some or all of their work from home during their workdays, while 82 percent did some or all of their work at their workplace" (bis.gov, 2020). This could be attributed to the fact that teleworking is not applicable to every job, or it may be due to a culture that reserves teleworking programs for just the highly compensated. It could also possibly be due to the fact that employees tend to work more hours when they work from their employer's place of business.

According to the U.S. Bureau of Labor and Statistics, (2020), "on average, employees who worked at their workplace worked for 7.9 hours, while those who worked at home did so for 3.3 hours." However, working for 7.9 hours may not equate to being productive that entire time.

We can inspire others to connect teleworking to their sense of purpose by leaving our egos at the door. The US Department of Labor describes a great method for accomplishing this. Leaders are recommended to adopt a more flexible,

Implications for Hybrid Teleworking Programs for Regeneration and Sustainable Development

adaptable attitude. "They must shift their focus away from controlling the process, to facilitating the effective performance of the process, while promoting a culture of trust," (US Department of Labor, 2000, p. 17).

Leaders must also be willing to engage others on a personal level in an effort to focus attention on the core values and the deeply held values and drive of their organization's personnel. According to Hardman (2011), "this capacity to engage people at the personal level has led to the establishment of generative conversation and decision-making processes far more likely to eliminate unanticipated consequences. Herein lies the potential for engaging triple-loop learning or suspension of all previously held assumptions in order to generate radically new solutions to problems and challenges, defined here as third-order change" (pg. 198). The roles of leaders and participants include continuous engagement of other regenerative leaders, and applying the steps outlined in the Sustainability Pyramid to implement teleworking programs.

The Bureau of Labor and Statistics, (2020), determined that the following employees are most likely to work from home:
- 37 percent of workers who are employed in management, business or financial occupations
- 42 percent of persons who are 25 years and older, with an advanced degree

According to DeSilver (2020), the number of private sector tele-workers (approximately 8.4 million) greatly exceeds the State's and local government number of approximately 776,000. Therefore, teleworking is more common within the private sector.

Implications for Hybrid Teleworking Programs for Regeneration and Sustainable Development

The following is a partial list of occupations that are typically suitable for teleworking:

Table 2: (televa.org, n.d.)

Accountant	Contract Manager	Journalist
Admin. Assistant	Customer Service Agent	Lawyer
Appraiser	Data Analyst	Manager
Architect	Economist	Researcher
Auditor	Employment Interviewer	Scientist
Budget Analyst	Engineer	Telephone-Intensive Occupations
Computer Scientist	Financial Analyst	Transcriptionist
Consultant	Investigator	Writer

Implications for Hybrid Teleworking Programs for Regeneration and Sustainable Development

Social Implications for Hybrid Teleworking

Employees yearn for the benefit of having access to hybrid teleworking programs. They believe that reduced commute to work: Saves them time and money; gives greater sense of independence, and reduces overall daily stress levels. A study conducted by Owl Labs, explored how employees across the United States view hybrid teleworking as well as remote team meetings.

The study revealed: "83 percent of survey respondents agree that the ability to work remotely would make them happier. 82 percent agree with the statement that working remotely would make them feel more trusted at work. 80 percent agree that it would make them less stressed. 34 percent of workers are willing to take a pay cut of up to 5 percent in order to work remotely; 24 percent would take a pay cut of up to 10 percent, and 20 percent would take a cut larger than 10 percent. Approximately 90 percent of workers were in favor of hybrid telework for improved work-life balance; 79 percent for increased productivity and focus; 78 percent for reduced stress from commute" (Owl Labs, 2019, p. 17 – 24).

According to DeSilva (2020), a 2015 New Zealand study that examined teleworking after a series of earthquakes, found employees felt more positive about teleworking than team leaders, possibly due to greater responsibilities during times of crisis. In addition, approximately 80 percent of teleworkers reported a heightened sense of independence. This finding aligns with the needs assessment conducted for this project, as approximately 82 percent of participants perceived greater independence resulting from teleworking. DeSilva (2020) also noted that "women were less likely to report positive benefits from teleworking and are more likely to report social costs such as loss of visibility, reduced mutual learning and career development."

Studies have also shown that teleworking is not for everyone or every job. "While teleworkers may not be disrupted my other colleagues, the lack of co-worker contact may seem isolating" (DeSilva, 2020). There is also a lack of space between home and work. The extra time saved by not commuting may be consumed by having to work continuously to meet family needs, circumvent technical difficulties, and maintain a positive presence from afar.

Considerations for adopting hybrid teleworking programs will lead to concerns about workers' compensation for teleworkers who are injured outside of their employers' place of business. According to Quinn, Sweeney & Techau, (2020), guidance is being drawn from compensation cases related to injured teleworkers. "Courts from most jurisdictions analyze home offices the same as a traditional workplace where a determination must be made as to whether the injury arose out of and in the course of employment" (Quinn, Sweeney, & Techau, 2020). Compensation is based on whether the employee was in pursuit of employer's business or self. Examples of cases in which compensation benefit was not awarded, according to Quinn et al (2020), include the following:

- A teleworker who slipped on the floor after finalizing a report for his employer.
- A teleworker who fell down the stairs on his way to breakfast while holding work records.
- A teleworker who tripped over his carpet and broke his wrist while pursuing non-work-related matters.

In addition, employers may be apprehensive about privacy and data security. DeSilva (2020) recommends combating this issue by providing teleworking access on a broader scale and in anticipation of future disasters.

Implications for Hybrid Teleworking Programs for Regeneration and Sustainable Development

Economic Implications for Hybrid Teleworking

The COVID-19 pandemic has increased the need for working from home, and our nation is becoming increasingly aware of the concept of teleworking. "Given how important our working lives are to our economic lives, we must try to understand the workforce of the future," (Donovan, 2016).

According to the U.S. Department of Labor, studies have shown that teleworking, even when done part-time, saves employers up to $10,000 per year in reduced absenteeism and retention costs. Workers perceive teleworking access to be attractive and are incentivized to be more productive, which consequently boosts the economy. In addition to attracting more talent, access to flexible workplace benefits preserves employee retention, and increases their loyalty to the organization, (Donovan, 2016).

Teleworking will affect the transportation industry, as fewer workers will commute to and from work on a daily basis. Government agencies such as the Transportation Department will need to take this into consideration when building future transport infrastructures, and planning for additional bus routes, bus schedules and bus lanes.

Adoption of teleworking programs will also result in a lower demand for office space, reduction in overhead costs, and increased hiring capacity. Teleworking could be used as a means for saving on prospective real estate expenses, for instance, back in 2000; AT&T teleworkers avoided 110 million miles of work commute, as a result of AT&T's hybrid teleworking programs, which included virtual office labor.

Implications for Hybrid Teleworking Programs for Regeneration and Sustainable Development

Donovan (2016) has determined that people's consumption patterns will shift to match their work-pattern changes. People will dine in more, or procure food and goods from nearby vendors. Given that teleworkers would be spending more time at home, utilization of retail pick-up and delivery services (such as Publix' Instacart and Macy's curbside pick-up) would increase exponentially.

The entertainment and social networks would possibly move closer to home, for instance, big screen movies will be made accessible for at-home viewing through streaming platforms such as Netflix and PrimeVideo.

Implications for Hybrid Teleworking Programs for Regeneration and Sustainable Development

Environmental Implications for Hybrid Teleworking

Teleworking can be used as a viable strategy for regeneration and sustainable development. The U.S. Department of Labor (2000), has determined that congestion reduction is an environmental benefit of teleworking. A reduction in work trip vehicle mileage will result in a reduction of CO_2 being emitted into the atmosphere.
For instance, in 2000, "AT&T teleworkers saved over 5 million gallons
of gas. They also saved over 50,000 tons of CO_2 and 220,000 tons of hydrocarbons from being emitted.

A teleworking pilot program conducted in Hawaii found 93 percent of employees reported a decrease in the number of work trips, which resulted in a 29 percent decrease in fuel consumption within a year" (toolsofchange.com, n.d.).

Implications for Hybrid Teleworking Programs for Regeneration and Sustainable Development

Further details on AT&T's Employee Telework Initiative can be obtained at: https://toolsofchange.com/en/case-studies/detail/129/.

References

Caffarella, R. S., & Daffron, S. R. (2013). *Planning programs for adult learners: a practical guide* (3rd ed.). San Francisco: Jossey-Bass.

DeSilver, D. (2020, March 20). *Before the coronavirus, telework was an optional benefit, mostly for the affluent few.* Pew Research Center. Fact Tank Page. https://www.pewresearch.org/fact-tank/2020/03/20/before-the-coronavirus-telework-was-an-optional-benefit-mostly-for-the-affluent-few/

Donovan, P. (2016). Nikkei Asian Review website. Economic implications of working from home. https://asia.nikkei.com/Economy/Paul-Donovan-Economic-implications-of-working-from-home

Hardman, J. (2011). *Leading for Regeneration: Going beyond sustainability in business, education, and community.* London: Routledge.

Hyon, I. (2019, March 27). U.S. News World Report website. Making the World a More Sustainable Place page. https://www.usnews.com/.

Quinn, M.S., Sweeney, J., & Techau, C. (2020). *Implications for workers' compensation liability when employees work from home.* https://nyemaster.com/news/implications-for-workers-compensation-li/

Owl Labs. (2019). *State of Remote Work 2019: How employees across the United States think about working remotely, hybrid, and remote team management, meetings and more. https://www.owllabs.com/hubfs/Owl%20Labs%202019%20State%20of%20Remote%20Work%20Report%20PDF.pdf*

Sauppe, A., Szafir, D., Huang, C. M. & Mutly, B. From 9 to 90: Engaging learners of all ages. Madison, WI. University of Wisconsin.

Stenger, M. (2017, May 11). *10 Ways to improve transfer of learning.* Retrieved from: https://www.opencolleges.edu.au/informed/features/10-ways-improve-transfer-learning/

Tools of Change website. Case Studies page. *AT&T employee telework initiative. https://toolsofchange.com/en/case-studies/detail/129/*

U.S. Bureau of Labor Statistics website. Economic News Release page. American Time Use Survey Summary. https://www.bls.gov/news.release/atus.nr0.htm. June 25, 2020.

U.S. Department of Labor. (2000). *Telework: The new workplace of the 21st century.* University of Michigan.

www.ingramcontent.com/pod-product-compliance
Lightning Source LLC
Chambersburg PA
CBHW030916080526
44589CB00010B/329